Aggies, Immies, Shooters, and Swirls

THE MAGICAL WORLD OF MARBLES

MARILYN BARRETT

A BULFINCH PRESS BOOK

LITTLE, BROWN AND COMPANY   Boston • New York • London

First Edition
Fourth Printing, 2000

Library of Congress Cataloging-in-Publication Data
Barrett, Marilyn.
    Aggies, immies, shooters, and swirls : the magical world of marbles / Marilyn Barrett.—1st ed.
        p.   cm.
    "A Bulfinch Press book."
    Includes bibliographical references.
    ISBN 0-8212-2001-2
    1. Marbles (Game)—History.
I. Title.
NK6215.B28   1994
796.2—dc20   93-32150

Bulfinch Press is an imprint and trademark of Little, Brown and Company (Inc.)

Designed by James Stockton and Associates
Composition by Wilsted & Taylor

PRINTED IN CHINA

Marbles pictured on the following pages are from the collections of:

Joan Beam: 2–3, 16–17, 28, 30 (bottom), 34, 41, 61
David Chamberlain: 11, 20–21, 39, 53, 55, 57, 58, 59, 60, 74 (bottom), 77, 78, 87, 91
Lynne Chester: 96
Bert Cohen: 19, 79
Brian Estepp: 51, 52
Robert Fulcher: 83
Jeffrey Grey: 45, 47, 48–49, 56
Steve and Florence Nacamulli: 9, 13, 30 (top), 42–43, 65

Page 1: Seal beach balls and blue and goldstone aventurine swirls. Rolf and Genie Wald. Pages 2–3: Popeyes and limeade marbles. Akro Agate Company. Page 6: Handmade swirls. Jody Fine (assisted by Art Ramos).

Jacket illustration: contemporary art glass marbles by Harry Boyer, Dudley Giberson, Charles Gibson, Steven Maslach, Mark Matthews, Anthony Parker, David Salazar, Rolf and Genie Wald.

To David Chamberlain
with thanks for your help
and the joy you shared

Contents

Acknowledgments

I am indebted to many people for their help in providing me with the materials for this book.

In writing the text I relied heavily on the information contained in several books listed in the bibliography. In this regard I would like to express special thanks to Paul Baumann, Larry Castle, Marlow Peterson, Mark E. Randall, Cathy Runyan, and Dennis Webb. Randall and Webb's 1988 edition was the first comprehensive book about marbles.

Marble makers, collectors, and dealers generously provided the marbles I photographed for this book. Its size and scope precluded using all of the images. I would like to thank Harry and Wendy Besett, Harry Boyer, William Burchfield, Nina Paladino-Caron, Michael K. Hansen, Jody Fine, Charles Gibson, Jeffrey Grey, Mark Matthews, Anthony Parker, Marlow Peterson, Ro Purser, David P. Salazar, Lundberg Studios, Art Ramos, Shantidevi, Josh Simpson, Douglas Sweet, Rolf and Genie Wald, Geoffrey Beetem, Jonathan Winifsky, Love Marbles, Joan Beam, Bertram M. Cohen, David Chamberlain, Brian Estepp, Florence and Steve Nacamulli, Victor Levine, Cathy Runyan, Red Wilson, Lynne Chester, Vittorio Zane, and Vacor de Mexico.

Marble dealers Bertram M. Cohen of Boston and David Chamberlain of Santa Cruz, California, deserve special recognition for helping me with the resources and contacts without which it would not have been possible to acquire needed information and marbles to photograph. Bert is a leading marble collector and the major dealer in contemporary art-glass marbles in the United States.

Others who helped by providing information and/or marbles: Judith A. Gray, reference specialist of the Folklife Center, Library of Congress; Gene Mason, director of the national marbles tournament, Wildwood, New Jersey; Stanley A. Block, president of the Marble Collectors' Society of America; and Robert J. Fulcher, naturalist and director of the Tennessee State Parks Folklife Project.

Teresa Mallen's hand-dyed silk fabrics were used as backgrounds in many of the photographs. Annie Glass, Jackie Marr, and Lydia Broadstreet provided other backgrounds.

I would like to thank my agent, Natasha Kern, for her continuing support of my work.

I wish also to express my appreciation to my editor, Janet Bush, and her assistant, Kristin Ellison, and to James Stockton for the design of this book.

Contemporary handmade swirls

INTRODUCTION

chance visit to a flea market one Sunday morning introduced me to the dazzling world of marbles.

With a camera around my neck, in case I saw something I wanted to photograph, I strolled the aisles filled with drab clothing, scuffed furniture, and garish novelty items. A flash of light from a table ahead caught my eye. As I drew closer, I could see, sparkling in the early morning sunlight, hundreds of marbles.

My response was visceral. In an instant I was transported back to childhood. There they were, reaching out to me from the past: the familiar cat's-eyes, the transparent clearies in yellows, blues, and greens, the large, multicolored opaque shooters I had played with long ago. I felt an urge to scoop up a handful, cup them in my palms, and feel the smooth, cool glass.

I was surprised by the spectrum of colors — every hue and shade one could imagine — shining from the sacks, baskets, and bowls of marbles. A cornucopia, more marbles than I had ever dreamed existed. When the dealer told me their names, the sounds that rolled off his tongue were as rich as the marbles themselves: black-and-yellow bumblebees, orange-and-yellow pumpkins, multicolored popeyes and corkscrews. Hand-painted porcelain chinas, milky white clambroths with colored stripes, and red-white-and-blue peppermint swirls. Root-beer floats, onionskins, and clouds. And the most rare and valuable of all: transparent sulphides, with tiny white animals inside; and Lutzes, clear and colored glass suffused with gold flakes and swirls.

I realized there was something special here. I asked permission to photograph the marbles and took the dealer's card.

During the next few weeks, I visited the dealer, David Chamberlain, at his modest cottage, which was overflowing with marbles, Art Deco plates, and Depression glass. As I photographed we chatted, and gradually I found myself captivated not only by the beauty of the marbles but by their history and lore, to which David enthusiastically introduced me.

Over a cup of tea, I asked him how he became interested in marbles. He smiled and leaned forward as he explained, "I traded another dealer some salt shakers for a little red box of marbles. I poured them out into a glass bowl and just fell in love with them. You have to have a nice warm feeling about something before you can collect it. Now, four years later, I've got over sixty thousand marbles."

By the time I had finished photographing David's collection, I found myself experiencing the same warm feeling that he had gotten from his little red box of marbles. Because I'm a writer and photographer, my infatuation led to the collection of images, stories, and reflections that have become the text and illustrations for *Aggies, Immies, Shooters, and Swirls.*

Onionskin (left) and slag (right).
Charles Gibson

The preliminary research for this book took me in many directions. I climbed 254 wooden steps to the top of a hill in San Francisco to visit Steve and Florence Nacamulli in their huge house filled with antique toys. They are owners of a salvage company, and like David, they fell in love with marbles after they had bought their first one.

Steve's tone was reverent as he held an antique baseball-size marble up to the light. "Holding a sphere is like holding the world. When you start looking at marbles, you see that each one is different, each has its own characteristics, and that they are works of art."

I visited glass artist David Salazar's drafty warehouse studio in Santa Cruz, where he showed me his custom-built glass kilns and glassworking tools.

He animatedly explained the nineteenth-century French lampwork technique he uses in his glassmaking. With a torch, he melts colored glass rods, which he then shapes with pick and torch into the fish and sea anemones in his aquarium marbles. A display case in the studio sparkled with the iridescent blues and greens of these paperweight-size marbles.

I spent hours in libraries researching the obscure origins of marbles. I read that rounded stones and clay balls, the precursors of marbles, have been unearthed in archaeological digs in Africa, Europe, and North and Central America.

Little did I know on that bright Sunday morning when I decided to visit a flea market that it would lead me on such a happy adventure. Now, a year later, I have been in touch with marble makers and marble collectors all over the country and have taken photographs of more than fifty kinds of marbles. As I looked through my camera lens and brought each marble into focus I continued to marvel at their infinite variety of color and design and the inventiveness of their makers.

The full story of marbles is yet to be told. Research into their origins has only recently begun. During the past few years the first well-researched, comprehensive books on the subject have appeared in print. The reader who wishes to delve further into marble lore and history may refer to the bibliography that appears at the end of this book.

Aggies, Immies, Shooters, and Swirls: The Magical World of Marbles is intended to be a pictorial overview, with accompanying descriptions, of various types and kinds of marbles. My wish for the reader of this book is that she or he will, while turning its pages, find as I did that marbles are both magical and seductive. Unlike other things we come upon in life that may first lure us with a gleam of light or a spark of fire and then fade and disappoint, the simple charm and sparkling beauty of marbles inspires lasting joy.

Antique Handmade Marbles

Clambroths, Indian swirls, and onionskins

Hold a marble in your hand and you hold a piece of history. The sparkling, round colored glass in your palm is a descendant of the stone and clay balls that have been used as toys for millennia. The allure of marbles is timeless and universal, spanning culture, generation, language, and class.

Archaeologists speculate that the small clay balls found in the pyramid tombs of Egyptian kings were produced for marble games. It is thought that the Aztecs played a form of marbles. Clay balls have been found in prehistoric pueblo ruins in the southwestern United States, in the Classic period Valley of Mexico ruins, and in the northern plains.

The Ohio Historical Society has in their collection a series of steatite, or soapstone, spheres with incised designs which were found in Indian mounds of the Hopewell culture dating to A.D. 200 or 300. The five incised balls were found with the cremated remains of a child and are thus thought to have been used as toys.

In Ancient Greece and Rome, children played games with round nuts, and Jewish children played games with filberts at Passover. The Latin expression *relinquere nuces* — putting away childish things — probably refers to the polished nuts used in these games. Although most early marble games were played with stones and nuts, some early Roman glass spheres have been found in Europe. Whether they were intended for jewelry or served as children's toys is not known.

A second-century A.D. Roman, Athenaeus, writes of a game of marbles in which the suitors of Penelope in the *Odyssey* shot their alleys against another marble representing the queen. The first player to hit the queen marble had another turn, and if he was successful again he was considered to be the probable bridegroom.

Glass marbles are thought to have been among the many glass objects made in ninth-century Venice, but it is not until the late Middle Ages that the playing of marble games is again documented. It appears that by then marbles were known throughout Europe. A manuscript from the fifteenth century refers to "little balls with which schoolboys played." In 1503 the town council of Nuremberg, Germany, limited the playing of marble games to a meadow outside the town.

In France, *troule-en-madam*, a game in which small marbles were rolled into holes at one end of a board, was popular. The game traveled to England, where it became the children's marble game troll-my-dame. Another marble game, cherry pit, in which polished stones were tossed into holes in the ground, is mentioned in Shakespeare's work.

The popularity of marbles in England during the Middle Ages is evidenced in the town council statutes of the village of Saint Gall, which authorized the use of a cat-o'-nine-tails on boys "who played at marbles under the fish stand and refused to be warned off." A painting by Pieter Brueghel the Elder, *Children's Games*, dated 1560, shows, among the eighty games depicted, a scene of children playing marbles.

From what we can surmise, the marbles used throughout the Middle Ages were made of clay. It was not until the early seventeenth century that water-powered stone mills in Germany were put to work making locally mined marble and alabaster into small spheres. In time, carnelian, rose quartz, tiger's-eyes (imported from South Africa), agate, bloodstone, and other semiprecious stones were ground into marbles in these German mills, and the word *marble* came to be used for the stone, and later glass, spheres used in children's games.

In 1720 Daniel Defoe, the author of *Robinson Crusoe*, wrote of a marble player as "so dexterous an artist at shooting the little alabaster globe . . . that he seldom missed."

Painted clay marbles

STONE, CLAY, CROCKERY, AND CHINA MARBLES

Agates or Aggies

By the last half of the nineteenth century, marbles made of agate had become so popular that the word *aggie*, a nickname for agate, came to be used for all stone marbles. Quarried in the Idar-Oberstein area of Germany, ground in nearby mills, and then exported to America as well as other countries, aggies were often colored with black, gray, green, blue, and yellow mineral dyes. Sometimes the color of the stones was altered by heating. In Germany, stone marbles were called clickers, a name that is still in use. The marble mills of Idar-Oberstein continue to produce and export the best agates.

Antique agates were painstakingly cut and hand polished by skilled agate grinders, who chipped the pieces nearly round with a hammer and then wore down the edges on the surface of a grindstone. Because of their hardness, large aggies were the most valued shooters. Today, the modern-day machine-ground aggie remains a favorite of marble players; those with a bull's-eye pattern are especially prized. Each year an aggie is awarded as the prize to the winner of the national marble tournament in Wildwood, New Jersey.

Because there is no accurate way to tell an antique agate from a modern one, antique agates have not appreciated in value among collectors and are worth about the same as machine-ground versions.

Clays or Commies

Clay marbles were the least expensive marbles. Although many were imported to America from Germany, by 1840 they were being made in a factory in Ohio at the rate of 100,000 a day. Glazed or unglazed, they were colored in the tans, reds, and browns of the clay from which they were made. These marbles were also called commies, a shortened version of commoneys, because they were the common, everyday marbles children used for play (see page 79).

Hand-cut, hand-polished agates

Antique commies are still fairly common. Unlike many other old marbles, they are inexpensive and within reach of the average collector.

Painted clay marbles were also popular. Some with crisscrossing wobbly lines, wobbly coils, or circles were called rolled commies. Others speckled with various colored points were called bird's eggs.

Overleaf: Benningtons

Crockery Marbles

Most crockery or stoneware marbles are brown with a blue glaze. These are called Benningtons because their glaze resembles that of the brown-and-blue-glazed Bennington Ware pottery produced in Bennington, Vermont, during the nineteenth century. Although this factory did not make marbles and most Benningtons actually were imported from Germany, the same method used in making the pottery was used to make the marbles. Small clay pieces were rolled into spheres that were then coated with glaze and fired. A manganese glaze created the brown color and a cobalt glaze resulted in the blue color. Hastily made in large quantities, they are not truly round. To be considered true Benningtons, crockery marbles must have eyes, small circular spots that resulted from their touching another surface while they were still wet.

Chinas

Late in the eighteenth century, factories were built in Germany that specialized in the production of china or porcelain. By the beginning of the nineteenth century, some of these factories specialized in producing marbles made of china. Fine white kaolin clay was used as a base. The porcelain pieces were molded into spheres and then fired at high temperatures in kilns. Once cooled, they were hand painted and then fired again to set the decorative painting of flowers, leaves, stars, and geometric designs.

Chinas were also produced in America but not until the middle of the nineteenth century. Advertisements for them were carried in Montgomery Ward and Sears catalogues from 1866 to 1903. Among the least expensive marbles at that time, some flowered chinas are today worth hundreds of dollars.

Hand-painted chinas

ANTIQUE CANE-CUT GLASS MARBLES

Although researchers speculate that glass spheres produced in ancient Rome were used as marbles, the earliest glass toy marbles for which records exist were made in nineteenth-century glass factories in the province of Thüringen, Germany.

In 1846 a glassworker in the town of Lausche invented the *marbelschere*, or marble scissors, a tool that rounded a marble in one step. This invention made it possible to produce rapidly large quantities of completely round marbles, whereas before each had to be rounded painstakingly by hand. With this simple cupped tool it was possible quickly to form and slice off rounded globes of glass from glass rods.

The multicolored spun-glass rods, called latticinio canes, already produced by the glassworks for other products, became the favorite material for glass marbles. The twisting of the molten multicolored glass rods in the marble-making process created the sparkling swirls or spirals after which the marbles were named.

Except for sulphides, and a few individually made marbles, almost all of the glass marbles made in Germany during the nineteenth and early twentieth centuries were the swirls or spirals that are today highly valued by collectors. By the middle of the nineteenth century, swirls had overtaken stone marbles in popularity.

The making of a handmade swirl required several steps and could be accomplished only by a skilled glassmaker. A rod of clear glass was rolled across a grooved metal sheet on which were placed partially molten colored glass rods that had been heated in a small furnace. The colors adhered to the glass, creating a multicolored cane. The rod was then covered with a layer of clear glass and twisted and pulled. It was reheated in the furnace and globs of the glass were then cut and formed into marbles with the use of the marble scissors. The forming process involved pressing the hot end of the glass into the cup of the marble scissors and turning it several times. The scissors were then pressed together and twisted slowly until the rounded glass was separated from the glass cane.

Next, the slightly hardened marbles were rotated in a wooden barrel, where they gradually cooled and became more round. A final step involved picking up the marbles with an iron spoon and cooling them in an annealing oven. Ten to twenty marbles could be cooled at one time.

At the point in the process when the marble was cut off from the rod, a small tag of glass was left at each end. These rough spots, called pontil marks, show that a marble was made by hand. Each pontil mark is unique. They are valuable identification marks for the collector and should never be ground or smoothed down.

Swirls form the bulk of old collectible marbles. Sold for pennies when they were made, some swirls are now worth hundreds and even thousands of dollars.

Solid core swirls

Latticinio core swirl   *Divided core swirl*

Antique Swirls

Latticinio Core
This swirl takes its name from the Italian word for "net" and refers to the open network of narrow strands of milky, white glass that appears in its center. The number of threads in a latticinio core can vary from eight to forty. Close to the surface of this marble, there are always ribbons of colored glass as well. More than half of antique swirls have latticinio cores, making them the most common variety. Their popularity is no doubt due to the intricate, delicate beauty of their open-work cores.

Divided Core and Ribbon Core
These two closely related swirls make up about 20 percent of antique swirls. Both have ribbons of color near the center which spiral from end to end. In the divided core, the ribbons are narrower than those in the ribbon core. Both types of marbles vary widely in color and size and usually have an additional ribbon of colored glass close to their surface.

Solid Core
This swirl has a solid core made with individual rods or ribbons of color. Eighteen percent of swirls are of this type.

Solid core swirls

Lutz

Golden veins of jewellike glass sparkle vividly in these handmade banded swirls.
Aventurine, a yellow glass containing small copper crystals, gives Lutz marbles their
phosphorescent brilliance. These marbles were mistakenly attributed to nineteenth-
century master glassmaker Nicholas Lutz, a French immigrant who worked at
various glass factories in the northeastern United States. The marbles that bear his
name were actually made in Germany and imported to America during the late
nineteenth and early twentieth centuries (see page 35).

   Along with sulphides, Lutzes are the crown jewels of marble collecting and
are prized for their beauty and rarity. Prices for these marbles have skyrocketed
recently. Marbles now worth thousands of dollars were listed in an early 1900s
wholesaler's catalogue at thirty-five cents per hundred!

Colored Glass Coreless Swirls

It was not possible to use colored glass ribbons within a colored glass marble since the interior colors wouldn't be seen, or if they were visible, the colors would be muddy and unclear. As a result, colored glass marbles were coreless and were decorated with either bands or swirls of white near the surface or color applied on the surface as an overlay.

Gooseberries. Gooseberries are an example of a colored glass marble. They have numerous thin white threads distributed evenly around the surface of the marble.

Opaque Glass Swirls

Less translucent than colored glass swirls, opaque glass swirls are decorated with lines, bands, and swirls on their surfaces.

Clambroths. Clambroths, or clams, are among the most popular of antique collectible marbles. They take their name from the chowder-white opaque glass, known as milk glass, from which they were made. They characteristically have many thin outer swirl lines of a contrasting color running from pontil to pontil. A variety of clambroth most valued by collectors has a black or dark-colored glass base with white swirl lines.

Indian Swirls. Also called Indians, these opaque swirls are made of black glass with outer bands of colored glass. They were named by authors of a marble book who mistakenly claimed that the marbles came from India. Although they were probably made in Germany, the name Indian swirl caught on and is now in common use.

Peppermint Swirls. These popular red-white-and-blue swirls were made around 1876 to commemorate the American Centennial. Although designs vary, each marble was fashioned from a clear core of glass surrounded by a thin layer of white glass decorated with blue bands and red stripes. The most valued peppermint swirls have chips of mica, intended to represent stars on a field of blue. Peppermints are sometimes called flags.

Gooseberries

Clambroths (top), Indian swirls and end-of-day (bottom), plain peppermint swirls and peppermint swirls with mica (right)

Onionskins

Although this cane-cut swirl usually has at its center a clear glass core, it appears solidly colored because the clear core is covered by a thin layer of opaque color and then covered again by a thin layer of clear glass. Extremely popular and highly prized, onionskins take their name from this layering of glass, like layers of an onion. In contrast to end-of-day marbles, onionskins have two pontils.

The base color, usually white or yellow, was applied by rolling the clear glass marble in powdered glass. Accent colors were added by again rolling the heated piece over fragments of crushed glass, creating a speckled effect. There are various types of onionskins: single color, speckled, and segmented. Sometimes mica was added to the glass, thus increasing its value. Onionskins were known to exist from the beginning of the cane-cut marble industry. An early example, dated between 1850 and 1860, was unearthed in the excavation of an old privy in New Orleans.

Lobed core onionskin (below) and onionskins and paneled onionskins (right)

Micas

Mica was added to many kinds of marbles. However, the marbles called micas are those clear or colored glass marbles with no designs in which mica flecks are suspended. The flecks of mica in the marbles add sparkle and glitter when placed in bright light. Micas are made of clear, blue, green, amber, and red glass. The rare red micas are much sought after by collectors.

Micas

Lutzes

INDIVIDUALLY MADE MARBLES

End-of-Day

Made during the late nineteenth and early twentieth centuries, end-of-day marbles were fashioned from the glass crumbs left over at the end of a workday. Traditionally, they were not sold but were given as special treats to neighborhood children.

Although end-of-day marbles resemble onionskins, they have only one pontil mark. From this we know that they were not cut from cane but were individually made, each with its own pattern. No two end-of-day marbles are alike. To make an end-of-day marble, a worker gathered a small amount of glass at the end of a rod and rolled it over a powdered colored glass that served as a base color. This was heated in the furnace and then rolled again over powdered glass, this time the day's leftover scraps of colored glass, which adhered to the hot surface of the base color. This ball was covered with an outer layer of clear glass and then ground and polished.

The story of end-of-day marbles is also the story of a simpler time, when neighborhoods were smaller, yet rich and diverse — a time when a glassmaker could get to know the neighborhood children and take time to share the beauty of glass with them.

End-of-day marbles

Cloud

Clouds

Clouds, like end-of-day marbles, were individually made. They are clear glass spheres with bits of colored glass suspended within. The interior colors — blue, red, yellow, white, or green — are in the shape of a hot-air balloon and seem to float like a cloud in the transparent marble. In some clouds, bits of colored glass were set within other colored pieces and required special skill to produce. Clouds are rare and valued by collectors.

Another individually made marble similar to the cloud was the paperweight marble, made in the familiar rosette design of paperweights.

Sulphides

Sulphides are clear glass spheres with white or silvery figures suspended in their centers — animals, birds, human figures, and numbers. They were produced in Germany from the mid-nineteenth century until the end of World War I, and they may also have been made in England and the United States.

The sulphide technique was devised by an Englishman named Pellat. He made English cameos from china clay and silicate of potash by pouring the mixture into a mold and then firing it at a low temperature. The same materials and firing temperature were used for sulphides.

To insert the sulphide figure into a marble required two glassworkers. As one worker gathered glass on the front of the rod, another pressed the figure into the soft glass. Glass from the edges of the ball was carefully folded over the figure. The sphere was then smoothed and rounded on a marver, a wooden tool designed for this purpose. During this process, air would become trapped between the figure and the surrounding glass, giving the marble its silvery gleam that is so pleasing to the eye.

Sulphides were used in jewelry and given to children as toys. The rarest sulphides are those in which either the glass or the figure is colored. Along with Lutzes, sulphides — called by some the "Queen of Marbles" — are the most popular and valuable marbles among collectors. Because they are easily identified, they are often the first choice of new collectors.

In a 1972 price list, sulphides ranged in price from $25 to $90. By 1991, prices for these same sulphides ranged from $75 to $5,000.

Sulphides

Machine-Made Marbles

Machine-made marbles from the 1930s–1940s in a vintage leather marble bag

For many of us, it is the machine-made marbles of the 1930s, 1940s, 1950s, and early 1960s that come to mind as we recall childhood games: the click of marbles in a bag or a pocket, the precious beauty of a favorite immie or aggie, the joy and camaraderie of a game played with friends on a city sidewalk, a vacant lot, or in a park. These same marbles, charming, colorful, and unique, have captured the interest of today's collectors. As antique handmade marbles have become more and more expensive, some machine-made marbles have now become rare and valuable. Yet most machine-made marbles are plentiful, easy to identify, and within the price range of the average collector.

Toward the end of the nineteenth century, American entrepreneurs began to vie for a share of the German-dominated marble market. Early attempts by companies such as Iowa City Flint Glass and the Navarre Glass Marble and Specialty Company of Navarre, Ohio, to compete with German production of handmade sulphides and swirls proved commercially unsuccessful.

James Leighton, who founded and worked for a variety of turn-of-the-century marble companies, developed a new tool—a mold on a pair of tongs. This tool made it possible to create glass marbles that had only one pontil, the rough mark left on the glass when it was removed from a long steel rod called the punty, or pontil rod. These marbles, today known as transitions, made from 1896 to 1901, were a first step on the path to producing machine-made marbles.

James Leighton was the maker of the majority of transition marbles in existence today. The marbles he made were slags—

imitation stone marbles—and on most of them the pontil was ground down. Collectors with a practiced eye are able to identify other transition marbles, whose makers are unknown, by their pontil type: ground, normal, melted, bullet mold, pinpoint, and fold, the result of variations in manufacturing techniques.

The first truly machine-made marbles were manufactured by an inventive Danish immigrant, Martin Frederick Christensen, around the turn of the century. By the 1920s, machine-made marbles had supplanted the imports from Germany. World War I closed down many German marble mills, and they were never reopened. Imported German handmade marbles were to become a thing of the past as the twentieth century progressed, bringing with it automation and mass production.

The centuries-old composition of glass used for handmade marbles—sand, soda ash, and lime—is the same basic glass used for

machine-made marbles. Other ingredients are added: zinc oxide, aluminum hydrate, and, depending on the marble type and design, various coloring agents. In the manufacturing process, the glass is melted in a large furnace to a temperature of 2,300°F for up to twenty-eight hours, until it reaches the consistency of molasses. At this point the molten batter pours through an opening in the furnace,

Fischer jewel tray with oxbloods; these trays were manufactured in the 1930s.

Overleaf: Machine-made marbles of the 1940s

41

where shears cut the glass into equal pieces. These pieces move through rollers and cool rapidly, hardening into marbles as they are transported. They then drop into metal containers for annealing. Once cooled, the marbles are inspected, sorted, and packaged for sale.

For clear glass marbles, the batch glass is melted, then the color desired is added. Iron oxide is added to the glass to make it green, manganese for purple, gold chloride for cranberry red, or cobalt for blue. For multicolored marbles, a device in the furnace injects different colored glasses into the main body of molten glass before it leaves the furnace. For marbles such as cat's-eyes, chemicals and chips of colored glass are added to the outside of the almost-formed marble.

Billions of machine-made marbles have been produced during this century. Machine-made marbles reached the peak of their popularity in the late 1920s and 1930s, when competition between manufacturers made marbles plentiful and cheap. American manufacturers continued to dominate the marble market until the introduction of Japanese cat's-eye marbles in the 1950s. Their enormous popularity over the next decade caused many American marble factories to go out of business. By the 1960s, interest in marbles had waned.

Although it is not possible to show all of the types and kinds of machine-made marbles, the following pages will trace the early development of American machine-made marbles during the first decades of this century. The examples shown are intended to illustrate the most distinctive examples from the leading manufacturers of machine-made marbles in the twentieth century.

Slags of the type manufactured by M. F. Christensen and Son and later made and sold by Akro Agate Company

M. F. Christensen and Son

In 1900 Martin Frederick Christensen patented a machine that revolutionized the manufacture of steel ball bearings. Using the same principles, he went on to design a machine that would make balls from glass. As a onetime machinist in a steel forge shop, Christensen knew a lot about steel, but he lacked the equivalent background in glass. Between 1901 and 1902 he hired James Leighton to teach him how to make glass, and he bought Leighton's glass formulas, which became the foundation of the M. F. Christensen and Son palette of colors.

By 1902 Christensen had patented a glass-ball machine, and in a year he was making marbles in a barn behind his house. Christensen's marble-making machine was made up of five or six pairs of wheels. It took a team of two people to operate it. When marbles were to consist of two or more colors, it was necessary to melt the glass in separate pots of color and then pour them into a third pot to be stirred. A worker would then gather some of the molten glass on a punty, allowing the glass to drip downward over each set of wheels. The other worker would use a tool to shear off the exact amount of glass to make the size marble being produced. Each machine was designed to make one size marble. There were eleven different sizes, ranging from ⅝ inch to 1⅞ inches.

Although this machine may seem primitive by today's standards, in its time it was revolutionary. Ten thousand marbles could be produced in a ten-hour day, far more than in the painstaking, one-by-one production and finishing of handmade marbles. With this machine and the glass formulas he'd acquired from Leighton, Christensen in 1905 established in Ohio the first company to manufacture machine-made glass marbles. By 1910 M. F. Christensen and Son, with its thirty-three employees, was prospering. But its prosperity was short-lived. Natural gas rationing during World War I forced the closing of the factory.

National onyx and royal blue marbles, among the first marbles M. F. Christensen and Son made, and the most popular, were also the first truly machine-made marbles. They were copies of the more expensive German agates, which were the favored shooters around the turn of the century, and were an immediate hit with children.

National onyx and royal blues were so popular that Akro Agate, Peltier Glass, and many other manufacturers copied these variegated glass marbles, which became known as slags. This type of marble became a mainstay of the marble industry in America. Other imitation stone marbles manufactured by M. F. Christensen and Son were purple onyx, American cornelian, Persian turquoise, Oriental jade, and imperial jade.

Corkscrews. Akro Agate Company

Akro Agate Company

Established in Akron, Ohio, in 1911, the Akro Agate Company originally packaged and sold marbles it purchased in bulk from M. F. Christensen and Son. By 1915 the company was making its own marbles at its marble works in West Virginia. In 1919 the company hired John F. Early, who refined and upgraded Akro's marble-making equipment. His most significant contribution was the invention of an automatic cutoff of hot glass, which further automated the machinery by eliminating hand gathering of glass.

Large box of Akro agates, with smaller box inset in lid

Around this time another invention, the grooved feeder, enabled Akro to produce corkscrews, marbles with three and four colors. With no competition, Akro became the largest marble manufacturer in the United States by the 1920s. The company remained the leading producer throughout most of the decade, until the late 1920s, when Peltier and Christensen Agate companies began to compete with Akro for a share of the market.

Several marble companies vied to outdo one another in creating the most colorful and unique marbles. As a result, Akro produced massive numbers of vivid multicolored corkscrews, oxbloods, popeyes (see pages 2–3), moss agates, and slags. Akro reigned supreme until 1935, when the Master Marble Company, which had been formed by four former Akro employees, gained dominance of the market.

Although Akro Agate ceased production in 1951, the beautifully colored marbles it produced, particularly those of the late 1920s, are the most collected American-made marbles today.

Peltier Glass Company

Sellers and Joseph Peltier learned glassmaking from their French immigrant father, Victor, who specialized in stained glass. When a fire destroyed their Novelty Glass Company factory, the two brothers rebuilt the glassworks and renamed it the Peltier Glass Company.

In the early 1920s Peltier Glass began to make a line of marbles, producing brightly colored slags, swirls, corkscrews, and moss agates. It became one of the leading marble manufacturers from the 1920s to the 1940s, competing over the years with Akro Agate, Christensen Agate, Master Marble, Ravenswood Novelty Works, and others. In addition to its regular line of marbles, Peltier produced picture marbles, a popular series of twelve marbles that each had a decal of contemporary comic-strip characters such as Betty Boop and Andy Gump. Today these marbles are known to collectors as comics.

The Peltier Glass Company is still manufacturing marbles in Ottawa, Illinois.

Opaque and semi-opaque swirls manufactured by Peltier Glass Company

Christensen Agate Company

Five people, H. H. Culper, Beulah Hartmen, W. F. Jones, Owen Roderick, and Robert Ryder, founded the Christensen Agate Company in 1925. None of them had a direct connection with M. F. Christensen and Son, although it is likely that some of the early marbles produced in the company's first plant in Payne, Ohio, were copies of M. F. Christensen and Son's slag marbles. In 1927 the company moved to Cambridge, Ohio. There the efforts of Arnold Fiedler, a skilled glass master with a genius for color, resulted in the creation of some of the most beautiful machine-made marbles ever made.

Victims of the early years of the Great Depression, Christensen Agate went out of business in 1933. Because of its short existence and the company's limited capacity for marble production, Christensen Agate Company marbles are relatively scarce. Today this company's guineas, cobras, flames, slags, and opaque swirls are among the most valuable and sought after machine-made marbles.

Flames. Christensen Agate Company

Brown-and-blue Ravenswoods

Ravenswood Novelty Company

Founded in 1929 in Ravenswood, West Virginia, by Charles Turnbull, the Ravenswood Novelty Company produced ceramics as well as marbles. According to company records, Ravenswood produced around one hundred million marbles per year. Unable to compete with the Japanese cat's-eyes that flooded the market in the early 1950s, the company went out of business. Although Ravenswood made only a few styles, primarily opaque and transparent swirls, its imaginative use of color distinguishes its marbles.

The Golden Age of Marbles

The decade that spanned the late 1920s and 1930s is referred to by collectors as the Golden Age of Marbles. One gets a sense of how popular marbles were when one notes that West Virginia companies such as Master Marble, Vitro Agate, Alox Manufacturing, and Champion Agate went into business and made a profit during a time in America when thousands of other businesses failed.

In 1933, at the Century of Progress International Exposition in Chicago, Master Marble put on what was perhaps the largest display of marbles ever exhibited. It used more than 5 million marbles held in place between thick sheets of glass to construct the House of Marbles.

At the 1939 New York World's Fair, entrepreneur Berry Pink staged a special championship marble tournament. Pink, an Annapolis graduate, well-known football player, and self-proclaimed "Marble King," did much to advance the popularity of the game of marbles during the Great Depression. He sponsored marble tournaments and gave away thousands of marbles, boasting, by 1938, that his Paden City, West Virginia, company had made enough marbles to give fifty to every boy in America.

Marble King

In 1949 Berry Pink and Sellers Peltier bought the Alley Glass Company in St. Mary's, West Virginia. This company had made millions of purees and two-color swirls. Pink and Peltier renamed the company Marble King and developed a distinctive line of the brightly colored patch and ribbon marbles that were popular in the 1950s. Each marble had a colored patch and ribbon encircling its circumference.

The most popular of the two-color patch and ribbon marbles were bumblebees, which were black and yellow; Cub Scouts, which were blue and yellow; Girl Scouts, which were green and yellow; wasps, which were black and red; and watermelons, which were green and red. Many patch and ribbon marbles can still be bought for a dollar or two.

Bumblebees (top) and Cub Scouts (bottom). Marble King

Fluorescent marbles

Vaseline Glass Marbles (Fluorescents)

Some marbles have a yellow-green glow when placed under an ultraviolet or black light. This fluorescence results from mixing uranium oxide with molten glass during the marble-making process.

Fluorescent glass was first made in 1830, by a glassmaker in Bohemia named Joseph Riedel. He called the glass annagrun, after his wife, Anna. The glass was made by Baccarat in the 1840s and called cristal dichloride. Today this glass is patented as Vaseline glass, and the marbles made from it are often referred to by that name. *Lemonade* and *limeade* are terms used to describe the yellow and green hues of these marbles.

Custard glass and Burmese glass are variations of Vaseline glass. Custard glass is a creamy yellow opaque glass to which bone ash and sodium chloride have been added. Burmese glass is a type of custard glass with gold chloride mixed in. The gold chloride causes the glass to turn red.

There are several types of fluorescent marbles still in existence; Akro's lemonade oxbloods and the yellow slags made by Christensen Agate are the most popular of these.

Cat's-Eyes

In the 1950s the Japanese introduced the cat's-eye marble, and the American marble market has never been the same. A clear marble divided by veins of brilliantly colored glass, the cat's-eye had a new and different look that attracted young marble buyers. It took five years for American manufacturers to discover how to produce cat's-eyes. By that time the Japanese imports had captured a large portion of the American marble market, and many American companies were forced out of business.

Cat's-eyes are still being produced by the millions in the East. They have been made in such large numbers and by so many marble companies that it is difficult to identify them by their maker. Since they are among the most inexpensive marbles to purchase, at present they are of little interest to collectors.

Cat's-eyes from Japan

Common Marbles

The machine-made marbles shown thus far are ones that are seen the least. Indeed, only 2.5 percent of all machine-made marbles are sought after by serious collectors. What about the additional billions of machine-made marbles that have been produced in this century? These are referred to as common marbles and are usually of one or two colors. They were less expensive to make than the more intricate multicolored marbles such as corkscrews, popeyes, and slags.

Common marbles, which account for more than 90 percent of all the machine-made marbles ever made, were manufactured by almost every company: Akro Agate, Alley Glass, Champion Agate, Marble King, Master Marble, Peltier,

Purees with a contemporary marble bag. Ravenswood Novelty Company

Ravenswood, and Vitro Agate. These marbles, which include solid opaque game marbles used in Chinese checkers and ordinary patches and two-color swirls, are of little value to the collector.

Clearies, another inexpensive marble, are as common as cat's-eyes. Also known as purees, they have no design and come in a variety of colors. Their bright, transparent gleam has made them an all-time favorite among children if not among collectors.

During the 1950s clearies were used to make "fried" marbles. The clearies were heated and then immediately submerged in cool water, causing the marble to fracture internally. The exterior of the marble remained intact while the interior gleamed like a cracked mirror. Fried marbles were used in jewelry and other crafts.

"Fried" marbles

Contemporary Machine-Made Marbles

Interest in the game of marbles began to decline after World War II. By the 1960s, once-familiar neighborhood scenes of children playing ringer or trading marbles vanished from the landscape as vacant lots and open fields gave way to real estate development. Mass distribution of television sets brought children indoors and radically altered the habits of play for American children. By the mid-1960s many marble factories had gone out of business.

Root-beer floats. Peltier Glass Company

Jars of machine-made marbles, including one jar of prized red slags

Overleaf: Toybox. Vacor de Mexico

People who grew up during the 1960s and 1970s are often unfamiliar with marbles as a game. They have never experienced that rite of early spring, when a bag of marbles was removed from winter storage in excited anticipation of the thawing of the wintry ground. A circle was etched with a stick in the softened dirt, and friends knuckled down for the first game of the season.

In the United States there has been a steady decline in the production of marbles. Five companies — Peltier Glass Company, Marble King, Inc., JABO, Inc., Mid-Atlantic of West Virginia, and Champion Agate Co., Inc. — still produce them, and of these marbles, many are solely for industrial purposes.

There are signs of a marble renaissance, however. Contemporary art-glass marble makers report brisk sales, and interest in antique and machine-made marble collecting is steadily growing. The Marble Collectors' Society of America has sixteen hundred members. It is estimated that there are twenty thousand collectors in the United States. Toy dealers report that sales of traditional toys such as marbles are increasing. Word has it that schoolchildren are trading marbles, and there is a general resurgence of interest in marble games and tournaments.

Since 1970, factories in Mexico and the East have dominated the machine-made marble market. Imports from the East are common marbles — cat's-eyes and clearies. The most innovative of the current crop of machine marbles are made at Vacor de Mexico in Guadalajara, which appears to be the largest of all marble factories. Five hundred employees make 12 million marbles each day. Twenty furnaces and fifty machines are in operation turning out twenty-six types of marbles in ten sizes. Vacor de Mexico's popular marbles have names such as glitter, sparkle, candy, galaxy, stardust, Jupiter, meteor, pirate, zebra, and flame. The factory ships to thirty-five countries.

Jupiters. Vacor de Mexico

Contemporary Handmade Marbles

Moon and Stars by David P. Salazar and Inhabited Planets by Josh Simpson against a background of antique handmade marbles.

In the 1960s as children's marble games faded from the American scene, another form of marble entertainment, that of collecting, took their place. This version was reserved for adults.

During the 1970s rare antique handmade marbles soared in value. Within a decade, sulphides and Lutzes were selling for hundreds of dollars apiece at marble meets and auctions. The contents of a child's marble bag, once worth pennies, became like precious jewels, stored in custom-made felt-lined cases.

On the West Coast by the late 1970s, at about the same time marble collecting was gaining in popularity, there was a revival of art glass. Sensing the interest among collectors, artisans who had been handcrafting vases, bowls, and goblets began making art-glass marbles. Since then, time, practice, and imagination have brought forth a fantastic array of new marble styles from workshops across the United States.

Some marble makers look to the antique and machine-made marbles of the past for inspiration; others, sparked by their personal vision, alchemize their dreams with the medium in which they work to reach new heights of invention. Many of their marbles are one-of-a-kind art pieces, definitely not destined to roll in the dirt.

The following pages offer a sampling of marbles created by contemporary glass artisans. The selection is intended to acquaint the reader with the beauty and variety of these new marbles, and share the inspiration of their creators.

Handmade Art-Glass Marbles

Geoffrey Beetem

This Athens, Ohio, artist designed and made wooden clocks before he became a glassmaker. He tells this story about how he came to make his stardust marbles: "We live in the country, where the stars look as big as silver dollars. One chilly fall night we all stayed up to observe a meteor shower. I imagined what these particles of stardust would look like captured in glass. After this experience I designed the stardust marble to represent one particle of space dust trailing in a meteor shower."

Stardust marbles. Geoffrey Beetem

Ro Purser

The tiny stars, hearts, and silhouettes encased in Ro Purser's intricately crafted marbles are made using murrhine, a technique invented in Egypt almost thirty-five hundred years ago. Murrhine-making reached its height in the nineteenth century, when French glass factories produced the exquisite millefiori, or thousand flowers, paperweights that today are valuable antiques.

Murrhine is made by assembling colored glass in the desired pattern in a cylindrical form approximately six inches tall by five inches in diameter. The cylinder is heated and, when the glass softens, is stretched like taffy to less than the diameter of a pencil and cooled. The pattern remains intact. The resulting "canes" are then sliced very thin, to be encased in glass or used as surface decoration.

In 1983, Ro Purser, one of the first contemporary marble makers, and Richard Marquis formed Noble Effort Design, where they developed innovative tools and processes to create their own advanced types of murrhine.

Millefiori-style marble. Ro Purser

Today, Ro Purser continues to make a limited number of murrhine and sulphide marbles, as well as art and architectural glass, on Whidbey Island, in Puget Sound, Washington.

Rolf and Genie Wald

Marble collectors and artists, the Walds produce a variety of marble designs in their Seal Beach, California, studio (see page 1). Rolf's own words best express the Walds' attraction to marbles.

> *Why marbles? First, the shape. The ancient Greeks called the sphere the perfect form. In nature it is the most stable form; water tossed into the air will become spherical. There is no beginning or end to a sphere, and they just feel so good to hold!*
>
> *Second, the scale. Genie and I both have Nordic ancestors, who were nomadic and lived in areas where they were inside for long stretches during the winter months. They produced highly detailed artwork that, for reasons of space and portability, was small in scale. Although we're not nomadic, we, too, enjoy making detailed, small-scale artwork, especially since our studio storage space is limited.*
>
> *The third reason we find marble-making so seductive is the infinite permutations and combinations of colors. Swirls and filigrees and corkscrews all spiral around the little handmade gems in a mesmerizing fashion.*
>
> *Lastly, we both possessed and played with marbles when we were kids. Just as they fascinated us when we were younger, they inspire us now. Losing one's marbles is another term for being mentally ill. As marble makers, we like to think we're producing precious jewels for a saner world.*

A fondness for the sea and a home within walking distance of the Pacific Ocean result in frequent visits to the beach. Inspired by the primary colors of beach balls against the neutral backdrop of sand, the Walds devised their popular seal beach ball marble.

Cameo-style glass marbles. Harry and Wendy Besett

Harry and Wendy Besett

Harry and Wendy Besett own and operate the Vermont Glass Workshop in Hardwick, Vermont. An apprenticeship in Sweden gave Harry expertise in traditional glassmaking techniques, and his exposure to innovations in contemporary American art glass give his hand-etched cameo-glass bowls, candlesticks, and marbles their unique style. Airplanes and stars became marble themes during the years the Besetts lived in the flight path of an army air force base. Interested in contemporary symbols, the Besetts create many other whimsical handmade glass art pieces using numbers, human figures, and letters of the alphabet.

Anthony Parker

Twenty-two years of glassmaking experience contributes to Anthony Parker's expertise. With a master's degree in fine arts from Portland State University, he has taught the techniques of glass art in Alaska, Oregon, Arizona, and Washington. His work is in the permanent collection of the Corning Museum of Glass in New York State as well as museums in Denmark and Romania. In 1984 a Fulbright research grant enabled him to spend two years in Romania, where he worked in seven different glass factories. It was not until 1991 that Anthony Parker made his first marble. Since that time he has produced many designs, some of them reminiscent of traditional marbles. Like many other contemporary glass artisans, he signs his marbles. They bear the imprint "FP," for Fulton Parker Glass, his studio in Portland, Oregon.

Stripers. Fulton Parker Glass

Shantidevi

A maker of glass for over twenty years, Shantidevi works out of her Kaimana Art Glass studio in Guerneville, California. She thinks of her innovative glass creations as her contribution to healing the earth. Her vividly colored, intricately designed "spheres of glass filled with glittering landscapes of the spirit" are forms she sees as synonymous with wholeness, "a reminder of our unity with all." Shantidevi's goal is to bring "some light, laughter and . . . order into a world that has lost its connection to a . . . sense of the divine."

The glass she uses for her spheres is base glass, recycled waste, which she purchases from large glass factories, melts down, and reuses. Her solid spheres also contain dichroic glass, a substance coated with thin films of titanium, silicon, and magnesium. Refraction causes light reflections in various layers of the glass, creating a fluorescent effect.

Dichroic sphere, Signature Series.
Shantidevi/Kaimana Art Glass

Angelfish aquariums, David P. Salazar (left); orbs, Douglas Sweet (near right); shark's eggs, Jody Fine (far right)

David P. Salazar

Although David Salazar produces a variety of designs in his Santa Cruz, California, studio, his most popular works are aquariums, inspired by his memories of drifting down a Texas stream on a small raft, gazing at the streambed. To produce the intricate, colorful angelfish and sea anemones in his marbles, he revived the decorative lampwork technique used by nineteenth-century French glassmakers Baccarat and St. Louis. With a hand-held torch he heats colored glass rods until their tips become pliable. He uses this molten glass as "paint" to form fanciful fish and sea anemones. As each layer of colored glass cools, he adds another to the design until he has built up three layers of color. He then immerses the design into a pot of clear heated glass and smooths it by rolling it back and forth on a punty rod.

Jody Fine

A visit to a neighbor's glass studio so intrigued Jody Fine that he himself became a glassmaker. Fine apprenticed to Richard Marquis in 1977 and then went on to establish his own studio. One of the first to make contemporary art-glass marbles, he was drawn to the form because he sees marbles as "universal symbols of youth, fantasy, and power . . . with billions of different designs and billions of different colors to work with." The variety of attractive, affordable handmade marbles for sale in his Berkeley, California, studio attests to this (see page 6). Although Fine makes bowls and platters as well as marbles, his trademark is "Captain Marble."

Douglas Sweet

Inside each of Douglas Sweet's handmade orbs is a small world made of multi-colored glass rods. To many, these worlds suggest underwater sea environments, but Sweet sees them differently. "I refer to each as a microcosm . . . not a planet. It's a little world you can travel into and explore." Sweet works out of his Karuna Glass Workshop (*karuna* means "compassion" in Sanskrit), an old converted barn along Bear Creek in Salem Township, Ohio. To make his orbs he reuses clear glass recycled from flawed glassware and colored glass rods imported from Germany.

He reheats the clear glass in his furnace until it is molten. Then as it cools, he rolls the clear molten glob in colored powdered glass, returning it to an oven when necessary to keep the glass molten. Sweet then presses the molten mass onto previously prepared glass pieces he has made using murrhine and millefiore techniques. Some pieces melt inside of the glass, and some melt into the surface. Finally, the orb is encased in a layer of clear glass, and after further shaping with various hand-carved cherry-wood tools as it slowly cools, it is tapped from the punty rod onto a padded surface. The pontil mark is then removed with a blow-torch, and after additional shaping the orb is placed in an annealing oven at about 1000°F to cool slowly overnight — essential to the process, since rapid cooling will cause the glass to explode. Working in this manner, Sweet can make twenty-five to thirty orbs in one day.

California Glass Studio

Nina Paladino-Caron and Michael K. Hansen have been glassmaking partners for more than sixteen years. Nina led the way, starting a glass program at a community college while working on her master of arts degree. She opened her own glassblowing studio in 1977, where Michael, a former engineer and metallurgist, joined her. Together they established California Glass Studio in Sacramento, California. They made their first marbles when Michael's four-year-old daughter asked for some.

Silver spiral twist, California Glass Studio (right); Venetian glass marbles, Vittorio Zane (below)

Vittorio Zane

Vittorio Zane's studio, tucked in a back street in the Murano district of Venice, was discovered by an American collector who had been searching for Italian glass marbles. Zane, a descendant of generations of Venetian glassmakers, makes his brightly colored swirls in the tradition that has made Venetian glass famous throughout the world.

Josh Simpson

An artist who has been working in glass for twenty years, Josh Simpson makes marbles he calls inhabited planets, examples of the unique ways in which contemporary glassmakers combine their creative vision with the ancient craft of glassmaking. Working with traditional wooden tools that he cools with water, this Shelburne, Massachusetts, glassmaker imaginatively shapes molten glass into an endless variety of fantasy planets. Embedded in the clear and richly colored glass spheres are continents, oceans, clouds, satellites — small dream worlds we can hold in our hands.

Inhabited Planets. Josh Simpson

Mark Matthews

This versatile artist was a painter and a sculptor before he became a glassmaker. Although he has been making glass for the past eighteen years, he didn't begin to make marbles until eight years ago. Regarded by many as the foremost marble maker in America, Matthews brings a vast amount of art and technical background to the medium. Through his seemingly endless innovative designs he has elevated the art of marble-making.

Matthews uses more than three hundred colors of glass — his palette contains twelve different shades of yellow! He buys every color available from one Bulgarian and three German companies. Challenged by the myriad creative opportunities glass presents, he produces sophisticated, varied designs in limited numbers. When he has explored the broadest range of color, format, and design in a particular marble concept, he ceases to produce it. When his limited editions of marbles have been sold they become "extinct," and are not made again.

Reverse twist onionskin. Mark Matthews

Jetson. Mark Matthews

Other Contemporary Handmade Marbles

Minerals

These contemporary mineral spheres, or aggies, are popular with both mineral and marble collectors. Mineral marbles can be made of many materials, including carnelian, yellow jasper, amethyst, bloodstone, India turquoise, agate, aventurine, rose quartz, and rock crystal (see page 87). They are very similar to those ground in German marble mills more than a century ago. Earlier mineral marbles are rare and difficult to find, while these contemporary versions, which are hand-polished in India, make an inexpensive and colorful addition to a collection.

Jeffrey Grey

Overlapping bull's-eyes reminiscent of stone aggies are the motif of Jeffrey Grey's fiberglass marbles (see page 91). A background in art, a job in the fiberglass industry making parts for antenna systems and reflector dishes, and a lifelong passion for marbles resulted in the creation of this artist-collector's hand-carved

Goldstones, hand cut and polished by Red Wilson

spheres. To make his marbles, Grey begins with a compressed block of fiberglass sheets. He cuts these apart and glues them together with various colors of dyed resin. He then hand cuts a cube from the glued block and with a belt sander rounds it into a sphere. The variously colored bands that give the fiberagates their subtle tones of color are revealed as he cuts through different layers of the cube.

Marlow Peterson

A marble collector as well as the co-author of two books on machine-made marbles, Utah schoolteacher Marlow Peterson creates contemporary versions of Benningtons, the crockery marbles that were common around the turn of the century. These contemporary Benningtons are harder and more durable than glass and are good for playing games. Their simple, rough-hewn charm has endeared them to collectors.

Peterson has had a lifelong involvement with marbles. He remembers playing the game forty years ago and recalls his father, who also loved to play marbles, baking clay marbles at home in the oven. Perhaps this is what inspired Peterson to begin making these glazed clay marbles for himself and then share the process with his third-grade classes as an art project. Using Peterson's method, the children roll clay into balls, fire them in a kiln, then apply the different colored glazes and fire them again.

Benningtons.
Marlow Peterson

Marble Games and Lore

Antique clays or commies

Chasies

OBJECT: To capture the most marbles and reach the end of the course.

SETUP: Mark out an S-shaped course using two parallel lines several inches apart.

ANTE: One each to begin with, but a handful for play.

RULES: The first player shoots or rolls a marble down the course. The second player tries to roll or shoot a marble to hit the first player's marble. If the player succeeds in hitting the first player's marble, or if the marble comes close enough for the second player to touch both marbles with the tip of the thumb of one hand and the middle finger of the same hand (called spanners), then the first player forfeits one marble. If this is not the case, then the second player shoots or rolls and the first player chases. The game is over when the players have reached the end of the course.

Rolley Hole: Part of American Folk Life

Two counties along the Tennessee-Kentucky border can claim the longest marble-playing tradition in the United States. In Clay County, Tennessee, and Monroe County, Kentucky, marble playing is anything but child's play. There marbles, pronounced "marvels" by the local residents, is a serious competition played only by men (although women challengers are honing their skills, they have yet to break through the men-only rule of exclusion).

The game played is rolley hole, described by some as a version of croquet. It is a centuries-old game, variations of which—called rolley holly, three holes, or holes—have been played throughout the world. Involving strategy as well as skill, it is played by teams of two on a 25-by-40-foot rectangular field of finely combed and packed dirt called a marble yard. Marble yards exist in numbers throughout the region since rolley hole is the principal sport. It is played each night during the nine months of the year that weather permits. The game is an important social event shared with family, friends, and neighbors.

So strong is the tradition that the rules of rolley hole have remained unchanged for over a century. Three holes are evenly spaced down the middle of the marble yard. The object of the game is for each two-person team to get their marbles in each hole in succession down the court, back, and then down again three times. When a player lands near a hole, an opponent tries to shoot the marble away from the hole. The marbles used in play are made of flint native to the area. This local flint, in black, gray, white, red, and yellow, is preferred because it is tougher than agate and won't chip or break in play.

For forty-five years, until his death in 1987, Bud Garrett, a local artisan, supplied rolley hole players with what are considered to be the finest hand-honed flint marbles. They have become heirlooms and like other favorite marbles are handed down from generation to generation. Each August the National Rolley Hole Marble Championship is held at Standing Stone State Park in Tennessee. The most famous rolley hole player was Dumas Walker. His skill at the game was legendary. When he died in 1991 he was buried with a marble in his hand.

So expert are the marble players of this southern region that their team, the Tennessee-Kentucky Sharpshooters, won the first international world championship as well as the British Championship at Tinsley Green in London, April 1992. To fill the requirements of these championship meets they abandoned the game of rolley hole in favor of ringer, the official game.

Flint marbles used for rolley hole

Marble Tournaments

Once celebrated as Marbles Day, Good Friday has included marble playing in England since 1588. The annual marbles championship, the oldest sporting event in England still in existence, takes place on Good Friday in the courtyard of the Greyhound Inn in Tinsley Green. This event is limited to adult players.

In 1992, marble dealer and collector Bertram M. Cohen helped to organize the first international marble tournament. It has been held for the past two years in conjunction with the tournament at Tinsley Green. Four countries—France, England, the Netherlands, and the United States—have competed. In 1992 a marble team from Tennessee and Kentucky won, and in 1993 a team from Wildwood, New Jersey, were the champions. Marble tournaments are also played in France and the Netherlands. Adults compete in a game called triangle in which players take turns attempting to shoot fifteen marbles from a triangle. The game is played in eight rounds and may last from three to four hours.

Since 1922, when Macy's Department Store in Philadelphia held a competition featuring seven boys and one girl, marble playing has been an organized sport in the United States. Marble playing became so popular in the 1920s and 1930s that tournaments were run by many local playground and recreation departments. Winners of these local competitions were sent to the national marbles tournament, which for many years has taken place in Wildwood, New Jersey.

Girls were not allowed to participate in the national marbles tournament until 1948, when a special division was created for them after they made a run for the title. Berry Pink, the marble promoter, dreaded a tournament victory by a girl. He feared that if a girl won, the sport would be labeled a game for sissies and boys would stop playing. In today's competitions at Wildwood, championships are awarded to both boys and girls, who must retire upon reaching fifteen years of age. The tournament rules specify that only the game of ringer be played (see page 80). After declining for twenty-five years, the number of competitors at the annual Wildwood tournament has begun to increase in recent years.

Presidents and Marbles

Many of the games that are today played by children were originally played by adults. And, although we might think that a modern-day marble-playing president of the United States had lost his marbles, chief executives of the past have taken pleasure in the game. Thomas Jefferson enjoyed not only playing marbles but also showing off his marble collection to his guests. American presidents George Washington and John Quincy Adams were thought to be players. One source describes Abraham Lincoln as a "marbles-playing terror," whose specialty was a game called old bowler.

Sulphide marbles containing portraits of Presidents James Garfield and Benjamin Harrison were used as campaign items. Teddy Roosevelt and William McKinley are also pictured in sulphide marbles. These are among the most valuable sulphides; a sulphide portrait bust of Garfield is worth thousands of dollars.

Blue swirl and patriot. William Burchfield, Cape Cod Glassworks

Other Uses for Marbles

Billions of marbles are manufactured for uses other than children's games or collecting. Here is a list of just some of their known uses:

- as reflectors in road signs
- as linings of spawning beds in fish hatcheries
- for graining lithographic printing plates
- as agitators to mix the liquid in aerosol cans
- by florists in flower arrangements
- by prospective home buyers, who place them on the floors to see how level the house is
- as an old remedy for snoring: a marble is sewn in the collar of the offender's nightshirt to prevent the snorer from sleeping on his back
- by undertakers to slide caskets into wall crypts
- in oil filters
- in pinball machines
- by fabric manufacturers to make fiberglass

Getting Started

Mineral marbles, made and hand polished in India

For those who would like to try a hand at collecting, here are some tips on getting started, including where to look for marbles, how to meet other collectors, how to tell the value of a marble, and a glossary of marble terms.

Starting Your Own Marble Collection

Join a Marble Club One key to starting your own marble collection is joining a marble club. You will meet other collectors and receive a newsletter that will list marbles for sale, the names of dealers, and upcoming marble meets and auctions. A list of the major marble clubs can be found on page 91. The Marble Collectors' Society of America, a national organization, is a must. The society not only publishes a newsletter announcing events throughout the United States, but also publishes its own books. Through joining one of the larger clubs, you will learn where to find a smaller, local marble club.

Develop a Library The bibliography will provide you with titles that give additional information about marbles. Many of the books listed contain illustrations that will help you to identify marbles that have not been included in this book. From time to time collectors' magazines or other specialty publications will feature an article on marbles.

Buy from Another Collector Buying from a collector who has extra marbles for sale or trade is a good way to acquire marbles and gain expertise. Through newsletters and marble shows you will make contacts with other collectors.

Buy from a Dealer Most dealers are also collectors; in fact, many have become dealers by starting as collectors. Some do business by mail order and work out of their homes, maintaining their own mailing lists of customers to whom they periodically send their updated lists of offerings. They may also advertise in marble newsletters, and most sell their wares at local and national marble shows. Although a dealer will need to make a fair profit, an honest and reliable one will save you time and be on the lookout for marbles he or she knows will be of interest to you.

Buy at Marble Auctions   Marble auctions are another source of marbles. It is sometimes unnecessary to attend an auction in person, as marbles may be ordered by the collector after viewing a videotape supplied by the auctioneer. There are, however, only three or four auctions that supply videos.

Specialize   Specialize in a particular type of marble. Learn a particular area of marble collecting: the difference between the rare and the ordinary, the basics of pricing. In a while you will be able to spot a bargain, and the knowledge you acquire will have general application for all marbles.

Put the Word Out   Have a business card printed identifying yourself as a collector and buyer of marbles. Pass these out to any potential marble provider you come across. Let friends, colleagues, and relatives know that you are collecting marbles. Chances are you will hear many a childhood marble story, and in time, as marble bags, jars, and boxes are retrieved from attics and closets, you may acquire some good marbles.

Visit Flea Markets, Swap Meets, Garage and Rummage Sales   Although labor intensive, swap meets and garage and rummage sales can be good sources of marbles at reasonable prices for those who have patience, enjoy the hunt, and know what they're looking for.

Visit Antique Stores   Although perhaps only one in ten will have old marbles, and those may be overpriced, the persevering collector can find antique marbles at good prices at antique stores and shows. It is a good idea to introduce yourself to antique dealers, as they often keep card files of customers who are seeking a particular item and will contact that customer when they come across the item being sought.

The Value of a Marble

Generally speaking, the larger and more unusual the marble and the better its condition, the more it will be worth. Any marble in mint condition will bring a higher price than a similar one that has nicks and scratches.

Size   Marbles range in size from ½-inch peewees to 3-inch spheres. The standard marble size is ⅝ inch. The larger the marble of a given type the more it will be worth (with the exception of peewees, which are worth more than the ⅝-inch-size marbles). A ½-inch antique handmade clambroth may be worth $100, while its 2¼-inch counterpart can sell for as much as $4,500. A machine-made slag worth $3 in a ⅝-inch version increases to $75 in a 1¼-inch size.

Age   The age of a marble is not as important as one might think in determining its value. It is less likely that older marbles will have survived in good condition. Also, even if a marble is documented as being hundreds of years old, if it is of nondescript clay or stone it will be worth little. A newer machine-made marble produced in limited quantities may be much more valuable.

Supply and Demand   As with other goods for sale, short supply and high demand will push up prices. However, scarcity of a marble doesn't always increase its worth. Demand among collectors for a certain marble, even though it may be plentiful, will increase the value, and in cases where a marble is rare and there is no demand, the price will be low.

Prices of Various Types of Marbles   Antique handmade marbles can range in price from $1 for a common clay to $5,000 for a rare sulphide with two figures inside. Machine-made marbles are rapidly increasing in value. Some guineas are now worth close to $200, but some Ravenswoods and many other kinds can still be bought for a dollar apiece. Contemporary art-glass marbles range widely in price. For example, many of Jody Fine's swirls sell for less than $15, while a Jetson made by Mark Matthews sells for $1,000.

Marble Clubs, Societies, and Associations

The following are the major marble organizations, through which information about smaller regional or local marble clubs may be obtained.

Akro Agate Collectors Club
10 Bailey Street
Clarksburg, WV 26301

Blue Ridge Marble Collectors' Club
3410 Plymouth Street
Lynchburg, VA 24503

Buckeye Marble Club
437 Meadowbrook Drive
Newark, OH 43055

Canadian Marble Collectors' Association
59 Mill Street
Milton, Ontario, Canada L9T JR8

Marble Collectors' Society of America
P.O. Box 222
Trumbull, CT 06611

Marble Collectors Unlimited
P.O. Box 206
Northborough, MA 01532

The Marble Connection
P.O. Box 132
Norton, MA 02766

National Marble Club of America
440 Eaton Road
Drexel Hill, PA 19026

Southern California Marble Collectors' Society
P.O. Box 84179
Los Angeles, CA 90073

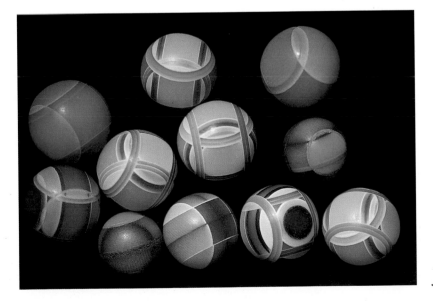

Fiberagates.
Jeffrey Grey

Glossary

The Language of Marbles*

The game of marbles has been played in England for at least four hundred years. The rich marble vocabulary that developed over centuries was brought to America by immigrants and remains, for the most part, unchanged. The names for marbles are reminiscent of Cockney slang, and they roll off the tongue with a charming, musical lilt: aggies, alleys, brandies, bulleys, bumboozers, chalkies, chinas, clams, clays, clearies, commies, crockies, custards, daubs, dobies, glassies, glimmers, hoodles, immies, kabolas, kimmies, marriddles, mibs, miggles, milkies, monnies, slags, stickers, taws, and twofers.

Aggies Usually made of agate, these are prized shooters, slightly larger than target marbles.

Ante An agreed-upon number of marbles that each player places in a circle or otherwise has available for play in a game.

Bowl To roll a shot on the ground.

Cane A long glass rod made of layers of colored glass.

Commies Handmade common clay marbles. Also known as chalkies, daubs, dobies, marriddles, mibs, and miggies.

Cullett Broken, leftover glass added to new material to facilitate melting in making glass.

Deegle A marble that goes outside of the game area during play.

Edgers Marbles near the edge of the ring.

For fair Playing for fair means returning all of the marbles won in a game to the owner at the end of play.

For keeps Playing for keeps means the winner does not return the opponent's marbles.

Histing Pronounced "heisting." Raising the hand from the ground before shooting; failure to knuckle down. Not permitted in play.

Hit When a player shoots a marble out of the ring during a game.

Hunching Moving one's hand forward while shooting. Not permitted in play.

Immies Glass marbles with streaks of color.

*A more comprehensive glossary of terms is available through the Marble Collectors' Society of America, P.O. Box 222, Trumbull, Connecticut 06611.

Knuckling down Shooting with knuckles resting on the ground until the shooter leaves the player's hand. Also a general term for the correct way to shoot.

Lagline In a circle game, one of two parallel lines drawn on either side of the circle (the other is the pitchline— see below). Players "lag" (toss) a marble toward this line to determine shooting order; the player whose marble lands closest to the lagline without going over it goes first.

Lagging Shooting to decide on the playing order of a game.

Lofting Shooting a marble through the air in an arc in order to hit a marble. Also called popping.

Mibs The game of marbles. A shortened form of *marbles*.

Pitchline In a circle game, one of two parallel lines drawn on either side of the circle (the other is the lagline—see above). Players stand on this line to "lag" for shooting order by pitching their marbles toward the lagline.

Pontil or pontil mark A rough mark left when the finished marble is separated from the iron pontil rod on which it is made. The presence of this mark indicates that the marble is an antique, since the makers of contemporary art-glass marbles smooth and polish the pontil marks on their marbles.

Roundsters Circling the ring to find the best position from which to shoot.

Snooger A near miss.

Shooters Larger-than-average marbles, usually of agate, used for hitting an opponent's marbles. Also called taws, bowlers, reelers, or monnies.

Spanner A shooting distance determined by measuring the distance between the tip of the thumb and the tip of the middle finger when they are stretched apart.

Steelies Marbles made of steel. Undesirable as game marbles, since they shatter other marbles.

Stick When a shooter's marble stops inside the ring after knocking a target marble out of the ring. The shooter may continue to shoot if he continues to stick.

Swirls Marbles with ribbon twists or spirals inside. Known also as spirals.

Target marbles Marbles that are the targets in a game. Also called ducks, stickers, dibs, and hoodles.

Taw line The marked line from which players shoot their marbles. The distance from the taw line to the target varies with the various games.

Bibliography

Baumann, Paul. *Collecting Antique Marbles*. Radnor, Pa.: Wallace-Homestead Book Company, 1991.

Block, Stanley A. "Marbles: Playing for Fun and for Keeps," *Encyclopedia of Collectibles. Lalique to Marbles*, pp. 151–161. Alexandria, Va.: Time-Life Books, 1979.

Carskadden, Jeff. *Chinas: Hand-Painted Marbles of the Late 19th Century*. Parsons, W.Va.: McClain Printing Co., 1990.

Castle, Larry, and Marlow Peterson. *The Guide to Machine-Made Marbles*. Ogden, Utah: Utah Marble Connection, Inc., 1992.

Cohill, Michael C. *M. F. Christensen and the Perfect Glass Ball Machine*. America's First Machine-Made Glass Toy Marble Factory, vol. 1, series 1, The History of the American Toy Marble Industry. Akron, Ohio: Group Ideate Publishing, 1990.

Dickson, Paul. "Kids and Collectors Are Still Knuckling Down to Business," *Smithsonian*, April 1988, pp. 94–103.

Ferretti, Fred. *The Great American Marble Book*. New York: Workman Publishing Company, 1973.

Grist, Everett. *Antique and Collectible Marbles*. Paducah, Ky.: Collector Books, 1988.

———. *Everett Grist's Machine-Made and Contemporary Marbles*. Paducah, Ky.: Collector Books, 1992.

Ingram, Clara. *The Collector's Encyclopedia of Antique Marbles*. Paducah, Ky.: Collector Books, 1972.

The Klutz Book of Marbles. Palo Alto, Calif.: Klutz Press, 1989.

Marbles: The Pocket Book of Marble Collecting, History and Games. London: Outline Press Ltd., 1991.

Randall, Mark E., and Dennis Webb. *Greenberg's Guide to Marbles*. Sykesville, Md.: Greenberg Publishing Co., Inc., 1988.

Runyan, Cathy C. *Knuckles Down! A Fun Guide to Marble Play*. Kansas City: Right Brain Publishing Co., 1985.

Smith, Linda Joan. "Lost Marbles," *Country Home*, April 1991, pp. 92–95, 146.

Antique onionskins

Index of Marbles and Marble Makers

A collector's jar of assorted marbles